PUNCHLINES

A Crash Course in English
with John Prescott

ATTENDED BY
SIMON HOGGART

POCKET
BOOKS

LONDON • SYDNEY • NEW YORK • TOKYO • SINGAPORE • TORONTO

First published in Great Britain by Pocket Books, 2003
An imprint of Simon & Schuster UK Ltd
A Viacom Company

1 3 5 7 9 10 8 6 4 2

Simon & Schuster UK Ltd
Africa House
64–78 Kingsway
London WC2B 6AH

www.simonsays.co.uk

Simon & Schuster Australia
Sydney

A CIP catalogue record for this book
is available from the British Library

ISBN 0 7434 8397 9

Typeset by M Rules
Printed and bound in Great Britain by
Bookmarque Ltd, Croydon, Surrey

'Some you it succeed, some you don't'

John Prescott, *30 December 2002*

INTRODUCTION

A few years ago, I found myself in a pub in central London. A young man at the next table recognised me, and said, in a friendly enough way, that he enjoyed the column I write in the *Guardian*, but why did I pick on John Prescott? Prescott, he said, was a working-class fellow who had struggled against considerable disadvantages and had risen to become deputy prime minister of this country. And what did he get for it? Smart arses like me making fun of the way he talks.

The young man warmed quickly to this theme. I pointed out that a great number of our most successful politicians had come from working-class stock. Jim Callaghan, for one, Neil Kinnock for another, and going further back, Nye Bevan and Ernest Bevin. They were all first-rate speakers; in Bevan's case he had taught himself to be one of the century's finest orators. They didn't hide behind their backgrounds, claiming that impoverished roots meant that later criticism must be the result of class-riddled elitism. The young man, far from being mollified, grew angrier.

I added that Prescott now held one of the highest offices in the land. Even if the 'real' deputy prime minister was actually Gordon Brown or Alastair Campbell, his job entailed tremendous responsibilities – for transport, local government, housing, and a host of other fields of government. No opera singer, footballer or even chartered accountant who failed to come up to the mark would be allowed to keep their job merely because they came from a humble background. No, said the young man, it was pure snobbery on my part, poking fun at someone who hadn't been to grammar school and university.

Nothing would soothe him, and we parted on bad terms. Still, I have little doubt that John Prescott would agree with much of what his supporter had said. There's a great chippiness in his make-up, a sense that others are quick to marginalise, ignore or simply mock him. He was clearly hurt when, in a reference to his job as a steward on ocean liners, Nicholas Soames yelled across the chamber at him: 'A whisky and soda for me, Giovanni, and a gin and tonic for my friend!' The problem for Prescott is not only that this sort of talk troubles him, but that he shows it. There is an element of the playground bully in many politicians, as well as in most journalists, and it is fatal to let the wounds show. You have to accept the rough and tumble. For years he refused to appear on radio or television with Matthew Parris, the sketchwriter who first spotted his extraordinary way of talking, and who first compared what he had actually said in Parliament with what *Hansard* later reported.

By contrast, when I poked fun at the impenetrable Glasgow accent of Ian McCartney, now chairman of the Labour Party, McCartney turned up in the Commons Press Gallery with a smile on his face and a funny book about how to talk Glaswegian. Perhaps he didn't feel so cheerful inside, but it certainly defused any tension.

Prescott loathes being left out of important meetings, and is constantly suspicious that the real decisions are being taken behind his back by people with university degrees. (He went to Ruskin College, Oxford, which is famous for giving a higher education to talented working-class people who never had the opportunity; but in Prescott's view his stint at Oxford doesn't seem to count.)

He is however well aware of his weakness: 'I'm not thick-skinned; if anything, I'm too sensitive,' he once said. He can also laugh at himself. In 1996, after a minor car accident, he had a routine brain scan, and asked, 'Did they find any syntax?' At the 2002 Labour conference, the organisers had hired people to type out, at great speed, surtitles so that delegates who were hard of hearing could follow the speeches. Even with people who spoke in slow and measured tones, the results were often hilariously wrong, and the experiment ended before Prescott spoke – or, as he put it, 'they've given up and gone home.'

In 1999 he caused a minor flurry when he said that he had become middle-class, by which he meant that he now had enough money to live a bourgeois life style. (And he does, in spades: there is the house in Hull, a grand affair known locally as 'Prescott's Castle'; the flat leased until recently from the RMT union at lower than market rent; plus a grace and favour house that comes with being deputy prime minister.) He has his own Jaguar, as well as a chauffeur-driven one that comes with the job – recent figures showed it cost the taxpayer more than £320,000 over nine months. The comedian Mark Steel once did a brilliant riff on Radio 4 the week Prescott caused controversy and jeers by taking his ministerial limo for the

200-yard drive to the conference centre in Bournemouth, in order to make a speech enjoining us all to use our cars less. His explanation – see p. 28 – did not help. Steel suggested that it was because Prescott had been raised working class that he enjoyed the experience so much. 'Look, Pauline, the windows go up if you press this button . . . come on, driver, stick your finger in the cigarette lighter, give us a laugh.'

Watching him in the Commons, as I have done for a dozen years, is an extraordinary business. Matthew Parris (and this is quoted in the excellent biography of Prescott, *Fighting Talk* by Colin Brown) records the look of utter dismay on the faces of the *Hansard* staff as they try to cope with the torrent, the wall of words crashing over them. He's fine when he's reading out a prepared speech or statement, it's when he goes, so to speak, off *piste*, and the words start tangling together, popping up at random, escaping altogether, evolving into bizarre new forms. As the following pages hope to demonstrate, he is creating an entirely new and individual art. I always think that a Prescott speech resembles a man taking a big and bouncy dog for a country walk. No matter how hard he tries, he can't help the speech racing off wherever it will, being distracted by a herd of cows, charging into undergrowth, tugging at its lead so it almost drags its owner into the mud.

His appearances on radio and television have also been memorable. He is a star of the *Today* programme on Radio 4, where he is usually interviewed by either John Humphrys or Edward Stourton. The answers begin by being grave and measured. Then they get faster and faster, more and more garbled, until the interviewer cunningly throws in a query about an entirely different topic. So, asked on to talk about, say, housing policy, he might be thrown a question on weapons of mass destruction. That's when the syntax crumbles and the *Today* team ducks under the table.

Ed Stourton, who really is a public schoolboy, told me he was usually given the Prescott interview, because it amused the then editor of the programme, Rod Liddle. 'It was his idea of a social engineering type joke to give me the Prescott slot whenever it came up.

'I got him in a corner a couple of times by persisting with the straight left – then in one memorable interview he came out of his corner with everything flailing. It reminded me of being sent out as a rather politely trained pugilist for Ampleforth against Newcastle Royal Grammar School when I was seventeen – my opponent in the heavyweight class was the England Under-19 prop forward, and it took about forty-five seconds for one of his wildly and unstylishly revolving fists to connect, laying me out cold on the canvas.'

I suppose that at this point it's the done thing to say that deep down, you really really like the fellow, and admire his stand on the principles by which he has always lived his political life. Up to a point. I do feel that his later stewardship of our railways, housing policy and local government has included an awful lot of failures. One can decide not to blame him for going back on a promise to re-nationalise the railways – it would have cost an enormous amount of money – but I do personally resent the way the trains got worse while he set up numerous feckless bodies, including the horribly named Shadow Strategic Rail Authority. On the other hand, whatever your views on the fire brigades' strikes, he certainly handled that with great determination, even to the extent of losing a lot of goodwill among the trade unions for whom he had worked so hard for so much of his life.

And of course he's added some much-needed spice to the bland face of New Labour politics. None of us will ever forget the time in Rhyl in 2001 when he punched the Welsh farmer Craig Evans. I recall travelling on a well-equipped Conservative bus to see William Hague performing in Peterborough the day after the fisticuffs. I counted that Sky showed the clip at least 37 times in the two hour journey. Now you can relive that golden moment through the pages of this book.

PORTFOLIOS

John Prescott MP,
Member for Kingston upon Hull East

SECRETARY OF STATE FOR TRANSPORT 1997–2001

First principles

'I think you'll see that the confidence in the public transport as shown by this side of the House in that they think it is an important part of the transport system.'

Popularity

'I saw in the paper today, how many Transport ministers, Barbara Castle, they said, was popular, when Barbara Castle brought in seat belts and drunk driving, she was very unpopular.'

Word from the underground

'For example, the underground used to talk to me about there something like £12 billion of investment is needed because of disinvestment and that's a cost, disinvestment you know, lousy services is a cost to the passenger and if you can get a long-term investment we need to take into account how we can get the modernisation of our services.'

Things can only get worse

'That was by alternative governments, so don't make that particular point, but we are now actually taking proper, putting the amount of resources and investment to move what we call extreme conditions which must now regard as normal.'

Positive Prescott

'For the first time in 50 years, bus passenger numbers have risen to their highest level ever.'

Improbable Prescott

'If present trends continue, we will soon need a motorway 150 lanes wide between [London] and Leeds.'

Inevitable Prescott

'All have a contributory contribution to congestion.'

FIRST SECRETARY OF STATE
(*responsibility for* HOUSING 2001–)

'I am very keen on the built environment.'

'Can I also say that I note he says an awful lot about we're going to give this right to buy to the housing associations, we'll wait to see how they come up with the plans, he suggested at his own party conference it was new policy, it's not new, it was said by Mrs Thatcher in 1979 and I think it was said by the honourable – he leads the party – but the trouble is they weren't able to whipperite* for very good reasons because on housing and charities you have difficulties about the financing of long-term finances affecting those housing, very real problems and I'm sure that we agree with them, but it was good for conference, but it wasn't much action, it was an awful lot of getting the conference going – yes, I will give way.'

*Perhaps 'whip it', or use the Goverment whips to enforce voting policy.

SECRETARY OF STATE FOR THE REGIONS 1997–2001

'There are difficult legal complexes – our draft bill this House can take first steps, which is creating a great deal of social injustice in our housing situation.'

SECRETARY OF STATE FOR THE ENVIRONMENT 1997–2001

'My position is that I want to make our position clear . . .
the example in Germany is just one example, for example.'

The caravan rolls on

'The sustainable conference,* about which we discussed from Doha to Monterey and on to Johannesburg, and this is a global framework, we need to bring it back together in a complete frame, as indeed it was in Rio.'

War and Peace

'The global alliance I'm calling for is as much for peace as well as war, and these two things need to be done if we're to sort out this problem.'

*The Conference on Sustainable Development

INTERNATIONAL STATESMAN (ONGOING)

Standing in for Tony Blair at prime minister's question time in November 2001, John Prescott was asked whether the first objective of the war in Afghanistan was the removal of the Taliban regime.

'Our objectives are clear, indeed in reading the *Hansard* of yesterday, the Rt Hon. Member did ask about these objectives, they were confirmed by my Rt Hon. friend the Foreign Secretary, the objectives remain the same and indeed it has been made clear by the Prime Minister in his speech yesterday that the objectives are clear, and the one about the removal of the Taliban is not something we have as a clear objective, it is, but is, possibly a consequence that as the Taliban clearly giving protection to Bin Laden and the UN resolution made it absolutely clear that anyone who finds them in that position declares themselves as an enemy and that clearly is a matter for these objectives.'

'I met that the Nigerian leader, er. The Nigerian leader, and he said that when he pulls the levers nothing happens, so we need a better form of governess* . . . a governess is something we ought to be talking about.'

*Perhaps 'governance'.

PRESCOTT AT WORK

The kind of decision he favours – 25 September 2000

'We shall make a decisive decision!'

Eternal truth – 18 March 2003

'That's precisely true now and more so this four more years on.'

Unfailing failure – 31 December 2002

John Humphrys: Does it worry you that a lot of expectations haven't been met?

JP: Well, it does if it was a lot. I mean our judgment of, often it's reflected in targets and there's a lot of attention to whether the target's actually achieved. Sometimes it only fails by 2 per cent and that's considered to be a failure . . . I was critical of targets when they first came in because I think if you fail to achieve them by 1 or 2 per cent the media will interpret that as failure. That's what I was saying years ago, and unfortunately it's still the case . . . targets are a way of how you can improve delivery when the electorate were not believing governments who were making promises and then aren't delivered.

Cycle of crime – 9 February 2001

'But you know we've achieved all of them. Only one of them – and don't forget this is a five-year programme, we've achieved it in some parts of the country – as to whether the fast track on criminal education from which you're caught and to when you're sentenced.'

Clarifying the euro – 9 February 2001

'The Prime Minister has made clear, when he was asked about this, that in fact a decision about the Europe and the consultations would be in the early part of the parliament, he's now defined it in that it could be in that two-year period when we will use the criteria established by the Chancellor for which governments will assess whether that's been achieved. I don't think anything has changed in that sense.'

. . . and again – 31 December 2001

'What we've done is actually expressed the political and economic developments taking place in Europe now manifestated by the euro itself. So to that extent I think we can see considerable agreement in the political discussions on the way.'

. . . and again – 17 May 2003

'Both Gordon Brown and indeed Tony Blair, and I think
in the statement they've reiterated how long ago they were
making these statements, that if the assessments are right
they believe we should go in [to the euro] and that's both
the same for Gordon as it is for Tony.'

On taking a ministerial limo for the 100-yard trip to the conference centre where he was to make a speech on the need to use cars less – 29 September 1999

'It was a bit windy, and the wife doesn't like getting her hair blown about.'

Against facts – 30 May 2002

'I'm asking you, if I gave you these facts, you're supposed
to give some factual analysis to it – I mean, you're not
denying that these facts are wrong, are you?'

Man of the people

In his biography of Prescott, Colin Brown records that while making a short TV film at Kings Cross station, a man reeled past waving a can of cider

Man: That's a nice silk tie you have on, comrade!
Prescott: If you don't get out of this shot, I'll stick one on your chin.

PRESCOTT AT PLAY

Do this, do it for our children – 3 October 1997

'During the election I met this chap who said, 'You've got to help me John. I've never had sex under a Labour government.' If you're listening, mate, I hope the first hundred days were good for you!'

On Labour pollster Philip Gould – August 2000

All that glitters isn't Gould.

On Peter Mandelson, near the Millennium Dome –
18 August 1998

'You know what his name is? He's called Peter. Do you think you will get the executive, Peter?'

*On the courtesy shown by the various candidates for
Deputy Leader of the Labour party – June 1994*

'We're in danger of loving ourselves to death.'

PRESCOTT APOCRYPHA

Deciding policy

'The green belt is a Labour policy, and we intend to build on it.'

On landing at an airport after a bumpy ride

'It's great to be back on the terra cotta.'

PRESCOTT ON PEOPLE

On Stephen Byers, the transport secretary who resigned after being attacked by a select committee – 30 May 2002

'It's true, they made a savage attack in words, and language.'

On Peter Mandelson – 9 February 2001

'He made the decision as to why he felt that he resigned, because there was some statement he felt some misleading.'

On Clare Short

When she was in favour – 17 October 2001

'Clare Short has made these points very clear publicly, in the Cabinet and elsewhere, and she's a dotty* advocate, let's face it, of dealing with this problem.'

. . . and when she wasn't – 31 December 2002

'She said that the Government is good in its substance, and then goes on to say presentation is crummily and lousy. Well, what do you want?'

*Perhaps 'doughty'.

On the Prime Minister – 9 February 2001

'Now, give over John, even the prime minister has done a lot more to do.'

'Blair scares the life out of the Tories. And me.'

On Harriet Harman in June 1998, after he was asked to defend her decision to send her child to a selective school, then against Labour policy.

'I'm not going to defend any fucking hypocrites.'

On the Conservative administration under John Major's government

'Here we have a government disintegrating between our eyes.'

And again – 18 November 1999

'We are unpacking the damage they have done.'

On William Hague – 28 September 1998

'Tory froth! "I drank 14 pints a day!" Our beer mat is unequivocal. Australians wouldn't give a XXXX for . . . sorry, comrades, wrong side.'

On the opposition in general – 28 October 1998

'The time has come to splatter the Tories!'

On Iain Duncan Smith – 31 December 2002

'I mean, IDS – cor blimey, he's the man – what did he say? – 'unite or die'? – I think it's more likely to be 'Die Another Day' the way he's going.'

Modest Prescott – April 1996

'I always have a problem with my face; I have to live with it.'

'If Labour gets in, I'd never get near being prime minister – I don't have it in me.'

Does he swear an oath of allegiance when taking his seat?

'I don't say it, I mumble it. It's one of my little compromises.'

Does an MP's salary make one middle class?

'I have changed. I no longer keep the coal in the bath. I keep it in the bidet.'

*When accused of overbearingly masculine behaviour
by the female French environment minister –
November 2001*

'Macho man, moi?'

PRESCOTT AND THE PRESS

7 March 2000

JP: Bear in mind that it's something like 70 to 80 per cent of the actual demand are single-parent households or single youngsters or people who are living in a single house – can we do that again?

People who are living in a single house – can we do that again? I made that crap.

Nick Robinson: We are actually live at the moment.

13 April 1997

Interviewer: You can't tell the truth all the time, can you?

JP: No, nobody does.

*18 March 2003**

JP: I don't know who Lord Hunt is, he's obviously a minister of government . . .

John Humphrys: He's a minister of health.

JP: Yes, I had to look him up.

JH: He's been in the post for four years!

JP: Yes, that may be so – [mock apologetic voice] – sorry for my ignorance, John.

*It is worth reminding readers that John Prescott was at the time – and still is – Deputy Prime Minister

31 October 2002

To Edward Stourton

'You're a terrible man for asking the questions and not giving an answer.'

PRESCOTT FOR POSTERITY

The Deputy Prime Minister in Hansard

Hansard explained

The *Hansard* reporters have the job of recording every word that is uttered in the Chamber of the House of Commons. Normally this is a routine business of taking it down in shorthand or on a patented Palantype machine, assisted by a tape recording to check doubtful passages. The speeches are then written up, and any problems (often involving proper names, technical terms and foreign words – once Gerry Fitt's line 'I have recently had talks in Dublin with the Taoiseach' became 'I have recently had talks in a Dublin teashop') – are sorted out with the MP or his office.

Hansard is not, as people sometimes imagine, a record of what MPs actually said. It is smartened up. However, MPs are not allowed merely to change their minds. If something they've uttered turns out to be untrue, misleading, embarrassing or against party policy, tough. But if it is simply ungrammatical, or lacking in punctuation, or meaningless gobbledygook, then the *Hansard* people will be happy to tidy it up and square it away.

For this reason, John Prescott is their worst nightmare. It is usually possible for us sitting in the gallery to gain a broad sense of what he means – firemen are paid enough, the government has consulted widely, the railway network is improving, and so forth. But the specific meaning of each line can be almost impossible to discern. For this reason, the *Hansard* people use tape recordings of Prescott speeches as training programmes for their new staff.

Here are some of Prescott's speeches as they were recorded on tape at the time, and as they appeared, bright and shining, in next day's *Hansard*.*

\

*The first two and the last were gathered by my colleague Matthew Parris back in May 1992, when Prescott was still in opposition.

John Prescott says – 18 May 1992

The Heathrow Paddington seems to be failing about because British Rail can't get the money for the 20 per cent required to get in with the private sector. The Olympia & York seems to be in serious difficulties because of possible bankruptcy situations in these matters and can't raise the money.

Hansard says

The Heathrow to Paddington link is collapsing because BR cannot get its 20 per cent with the private sector investment that is required. Olympia & York appears to be bankrupt and cannot raise money.

John Prescott says – 18 May 1992

I mean that's an example of this Government that believes in the private sector and is in fact damaged the public sector's handling within the public sector in a number of these areas and you can go on with them in another areas.

Hansard says

The Government's insistence on private sector terms has
damaged the public sector.

John Prescott says – 18 July 2002

I think that we are prepared to tolerate that, because it's not a policy difference only, it's all those people who haven't got homes, the doctors and nurses, the people who are in homeless, they're the ones who've been carrying the pain for that.

Hansard says

We are not prepared to tolerate that, because this is not a political issue only; it involves all those who have not got homes. The Rt Hon. Gentleman refers to doctors and nurses, but homeless people and those in bed and breakfasts are also carrying the pain.

John Prescott says – 16 June 2003

When challenged by David Davis, his Tory opposite number, over whether people in the north of England wanted elected regional assemblies.

They want to have a referendum, but nevertheless there's a county council here, he starts reeling through some of these people who are opposed to it, can I tell him I have some of those polls and by the way Mori poll, for example, in March 99, 99, that's less than 2,000, and many people actually accept the authority of these polls when they come out with their results, the Mori poll said 52 per cent want a referendum, BBC poll in 2002 said 72 per cent want it, and indeed council, council network, the very council councils who are opposing this, set up a review in their own area and 70 per cent of the people said they needed a review, they want a referendum and the county council themselves, they paid for that review and 70 per cent said they wanted a referendum and so I'm a little bit more cautious when I hear the Rt Hon. Member talking about it, and when you bear in mind that in all these referendums, Cheshire, they were part of the county council network [loud Tory jeers] well, I know you don't like results but that is what happened, that's despite what happened in all these areas we have shown whether trade unions, whether the business, whether organisations or individuals, they have called for a referendum and that has persuaded me in the three northern areas to hold that referendum, and properly so, and therefore I think that there is considerable evident to be taken alongside that which I have laid before the House today and as to the abolishment of council council reforms he made in his contribution, he must be aware that the Tory government has abolished more country councils than a Labour government has, and didn't even ask them, I know country councils have been abolished by them and I think I should remind them . . .

Hansard says

The hon. Gentleman means the county council, but others are involved. That is what the county council has to say. The Rt Hon. Member for Haltemprice and Howden (David Davis) reels off all those people who are against the proposals, but I have some of the polls here – for example, a Mori poll of March 1999 – and many people accept their authority when the results come out. One says that 52 per cent wanted a referendum, and one BBC poll of 2002 said that 72 per cent wanted one. Indeed, the County Councils Network – the very county councils that are opposing the proposals – set up a review in their own areas and 70 per cent of the people said that they wanted a referendum. That is the county councils themselves: they paid for that review and more than 70 per cent said that they want a referendum, so I am a little cautious when I hear the Rt Hon. Gentleman talking about them.

In all these referendums, Cheshire – [*Interruption*] – Well, it was part of the County Council Network. [*Interruption*] I know that Conservative Members do not like the results, but that is what happened. In all those areas we have shown that people – trade unions, businesses, organisations and individuals – have called for a referendum. That has persuaded me to hold a referendum in the three northern areas that I have mentioned, and properly so.

There is considerable evidence to be taken alongside that which I have placed before the House today. As for the abolition of the county councils and the point that the Rt Hon. Gentleman made, he must be aware that the Tory Government abolished more county councils than the Labour Government, and did not even ask them. He knows that those county councils were abolished by the Tories, and I should remind the Opposition of them . . .

John Prescott concludes – 18 May 1992

So I think the basic point that it is necessary in order to have private capital in our industries to get the extra resources that we do want that you have to be privatized is not borne out by the facts, in other countries, and neither we should we have it here also and if he's any doubts about that go and have a look at the reports that talk it.

Hansard concludes

Matthew Parris reports that *Hansard* gave up, and did not even attempt to report the last passage.

HIS FINEST HOUR

A Case Study

Prescott's progress through the firefighters' strike

In October 2002, the Fire Brigades Union announced a series of strikes. The Deputy Prime Minister was put in charge of the negotiations. The crisis lasted until Summer 2003.

***Different names Prescott had for the general secretary
of the Fire Brigades Union, Andy Gilchrist***

Andy Christ   *22 October 2002*

Mr Gillcrust   *26 November 2002*

22 October 2002 – The Problem

'It is true that we have been asked for, but the circumstances are such that we put it back to the employers that it's your judgment to make about the wage negotiations, and it's the same advice I gave to the local authority negotiations that were going on at the same time and were in a different situation.'

14 November 2002 – Initial difficulties

David Davis accuses him of an unwonted respect for the sanctity of the picket line

'It's not the sanity of the picket lines that bothers me, it's the sanity of human life!'

Asked whether firefighters had been offered a rise of 16 per cent

'It was hey-diddle-diddle, the man in the middle, it was 25,000 instead of 30,000, and we can see how they probably arrived at that.'

22 November 2002 – Attempting the impossible

He appeared on the Today *programme to clarify the situation after last-minute hopes of an end to the strike had been dashed by the government*

'Would you expect me to sign up or agree something at 2 o'clock in the morning when I can't see what the agreement is, I can't see what words have changed, I can't see what the proposals are for modernisation? It would be like signing a bouncing cheque!'

26 November 2002 – All the answers*

Should statutory law be invoked to end the strike on grounds of public safety?

'The agreement is taking place. I tell him properly that if his judgment to make a judgment on the public interest and the safety of the community. That is not my judgment, it is the judgment given to the attorney general.'

---

*In the interests of clarity, I have supplied the questions which John Prescott appeared to answer in a long speech in the House.

Should the TUC deploy their own agreement, by which the unions do nothing that might jeopardise public safety?

'As for the question about whether the TUC have agreement if the members of the 1978 agreement, that is a matter for the TUC and their agreement, but it is the matter for me to an agreement, as I informed the House, I did seek to find an agreement which I failed on the first occasion, dealing with this really exceptional in conflict.'

What should be done about pay differences between full and part-time firefighters?

'When I asked for – can't we have the figures? That seems simple to calculate what the money is but then you have to renegotiate the whole allowances that you then find out, that's not easy to do it immediately – I put forward perhaps one understanding.'

Will the Government use the law to stop London tube drivers taking secondary action?

'I've already mentioned quite frankly there may be a 100, previously, then it was down to one yesterday, now it's no, not. And I think we should welcome that as a fact.'

Why won't the government get all sides into one room and feed them beer and sandwiches until they agree?

'I think it's more wine and canapés at the moment.'

Why don't ministers make sure the military can use the 400 fire engines which are available but are standing idle?

'There are 400 engines, some without an engine, some without wheels, I mean, I don't know what you mean by that.'

Might the firefighters be more willing than we realise to adopt new working practices?

'I personally have always had that to my mind, and in particular for the consequences of fire service. I visited my fire stations. They posed the question of what is the work of the firefighter, and that precisely what we have to dress ourselves to this. That should be the front of every one of us. It's certainly to the front in my intentions, and I intend to see we can achieve it.'

Exactly how much had the firefighters been offered?

'In regard to the 4 per cent wage increase, that of course was for the first year, which was generally offered by the employers and indeed was referred to by the Bain inquiry. The 11 per cent, the 1.3, later the 7.3, to which you refer, added to the 4 per cent . . . the overall part of the pay bill is the 7.4 per cent!'

All's well that ends well

By summer 2003 the dispute was concluded by a white paper, leaked beforehand to The Times. *David Davis wanted to know why*

'Mr Speaker, it is unusual for a government spokesman to get up and say 'thanks for advance copy of the statements of the hon. Member', he read it beautifully, I have studied the questions and he read it to a 'T'. I thank him for giving me advance notice of his questions, but on a more serious point when he printed this, which I got a couple of hours ago, he was asking the questions about the press and he asked me to ring him. Of course I tried to ring him, but

he's a businessman, a busy man, and of course I tried to ring him, but I couldn't get through to him, but eventually we did a few minutes before we entered the Chamber and I did and I could have explained to him what I was going to explain to the House which I explained to him a few minutes ago, but it's nothing at all with any of the briefing which was in this white paper. We did not give the white paper to anyone, we did not brief on the white paper. There is nothing actually in these points in this story, but here in the white paper or have otherwise been mentioned in this House during debates and statements I have made in the past. And if I was to brief them one presumes at least to brief the papers the purpose is to get a favourable response. But since the headline 'Prescott takes the revenge on firefighters' I miserably failed on that, if that was the case. Though I believe the reporter involved has already apologised; that wasn't the intention of her story. I don't know whether it was or not; I don't talk to the press, quite frankly as the honourable knows, except to the motoring correspondents of the *Sun*. But I'll leave that aside.'

30 June 2003

'We shall reform the Fire Services Expectorate.'

On seeing the author, Simon Hoggart, behind the stage at the 2002 Labour conference in Blackpool:

'There's that bloody idiot . . .'